MW00856374

LEGENDS OF WARFARE

GROUND

155 mm Gun M1 "Long Tom"

and 8-inch Howitzer in WWII and Korea

DAVID DOYLE

SCHIFFER MILITARY

4880 Lower Valley Road   Atglen, PA 19310

Copyright © 2022 by David Doyle

Library of Congress Control Number: 2021942745

All rights reserved. No part of this work may be reproduced or used in any form or by any means—graphic, electronic, or mechanical, including photocopying or information storage and retrieval systems—without written permission from the publisher.

The scanning, uploading, and distribution of this book or any part thereof via the Internet or any other means without the permission of the publisher is illegal and punishable by law. Please purchase only authorized editions and do not participate in or encourage the electronic piracy of copyrighted materials.

"Schiffer Military" and the arrow logo are trademarks of Schiffer Publishing, Ltd.

Designed by Justin Watkinson
Layout design by Jack Chappell
Type set in Impact/Minion Pro/Univers LT Std

ISBN: 978-0-7643-6339-9
Printed in India

Published by Schiffer Publishing, Ltd.
4880 Lower Valley Road
Atglen, PA 19310
Phone: (610) 593-1777; Fax: (610) 593-2002
Email: Info@schifferbooks.com
Web: www.schifferbooks.com

For our complete selection of fine books on this and related subjects, please visit our website at www.schifferbooks.com. You may also write for a free catalog.

Schiffer Publishing's titles are available at special discounts for bulk purchases for sales promotions or premiums. Special editions, including personalized covers, corporate imprints, and excerpts, can be created in large quantities for special needs. For more information, contact the publisher.

We are always looking for people to write books on new and related subjects. If you have an idea for a book, please contact us at proposals@schifferbooks.com.

Acknowledgments

This book would not have been possible without the considerable help of a number of friends, including Tom Kailbourn, Jim Gilmore, Dana Bell, Scott Taylor, John Charvat, Chris Hughes, John Blackman, Steve Zaloga, and Gordon Blaker. Of course, my amazing wife, Denise, worked side by side with me on this project, copying countless documents and images and providing ongoing encouragement.

All photos not otherwise credited are from the collections of the National Archives and Records Administration.

Contents

Introduction

The US Army has long felt that two distinct types of field artillery were needed—direct-fire weapons, termed guns, and indirect-fire weapons, known as howitzers. The projectile of a gun is comparatively small, with a large propellant charge, and moves at a high velocity along the line of sight. The howitzer projectile is large, with a smaller propellant charge and lower velocity, and moves on a high trajectory with a steep angle of descent. Each type of weapon fulfills similar yet different specific tactical roles.

While not the largest, the most abundant heavy artillery used by the US Army during World War II were the 155 mm guns M1, M1A1, and M2, commonly known as the "Long Tom," along with the companion indirect-fire weapon, the 8-inch howitzer M1. These weapons, although having a total production of only about 3,000 units, formed the cornerstone for the Army's divisional artillery during World War II and, even today, are among the most-recognized field artillery pieces in the world. First seeing combat in World War II, both pieces served well beyond that conflict, performing equally effectively in the Korean War, and remaining in service for decades longer, redesignated as the M59 155 mm gun and M115 8-inch howitzer.

Through the United States' involvement in World War I, the US Army began using the Canon de 155 mm Grande Puissance Filloux (GPF), which was adopted by the US as the M1917 and in fact was license-produced by US manufacturers as the M1918M1. Initially, 2,000 of the US-built versions were ordered, but due to the Armistice, the orders were cut to 880 (these in addition to the French-built weapons purchased by the Americans).

While none of the US-produced guns made it to Europe for the Great War, both the French- and US-built weapons remained in the US arsenal for some time, to the extent that 973 were in US stocks as of June 1940. Arguably, the most significant impact of those guns was the establishment, in the US, of the manufacturing base necessary to produce them, in particular the recuperator.

The recuperator, or recoil mechanism, absorbs the recoil of the weapon and returns the gun to position after firing, preventing the weapon from "leaping out of aim at each discharge." An Ordnance Department report on this states, "The forging, boring, reinforcing, machining, residual stressing, and finishing the gun body itself is not half the battle of manufacturing. It is scarcely one-third of it. In addition, the design and manufacture of adequate carriages presents engineering problems of the most baffling sort. ... It is an understatement to say that a modern hydro-pneumatic recuperator must be finished with the precision of a watch." No *heavy* articles ever before turned out in American workshops required in their finish the degree of microscopic perfection the recuperators demanded.

The M1918M1 guns were typically mounted on M1917 or M1917A1 carriages, which were intended for low-speed towing. Per actions of the Ordnance Committee in April 1937, these carriages were modified with roller bearings, pneumatic rubber tires, and electric brakes, making them suitable for high-speed towing. The modified carriages were classified M1917A1 and M1918A1. The carriages that were not modified were reclassified as "limited standard."

From World War I until World War II, the US Army used the M1917- and M1918-series 155 mm guns, based on a French design. Here, an M1917 or M1918 155 mm gun has been unloaded from a railroad car at Alexandria, Louisiana, around 1941.

A 155 mm gun is being unloaded from a railroad car at Alexandria, Louisiana. The M1917 155 mm guns were of French manufacture, while the M1918s were built in America. The detachable spades are stored on the rears of the trails.

CHAPTER 1
The New Generation of Guns

In May 1919, the US Army Caliber Board described the envisioned future "ideal gun" in this way:

A caliber of about 155 mm on a carriage permitting a vertical fire arc from 0° to plus 65° with a horizontal arc of fire of 360°.

A projectile weighing not over 100 pounds which should be interchangeable with that provided for the Corps Howitzer. High explosive shell only should be furnished. The self-propelled caterpillar unit offers a promising field of development for this type of gun, but a certain proportion should be retained on rubber-tired-wheeled mounts for rapid transportation. The maximum speed for the former type should be 6 miles per hour and for the latter type 12 miles per hour.

Ammunition should be carried in original containers, in trucks and tractor caissons. The conventional type of caisson is considered uneconomical and is obsolete for this caliber. The maximum range should be about 25,000 yards. A normal charge for range of 18,000 yards should be provided with supercharge for greater ranges.

The GPF and M1918M1 had a range of 17,700 yards and had been outranged by the German 150 mm gun, whose range was approximately 23,000 yards, thus driving the US desire for a 25,000-yard range.

At the same time, it was proposed that a companion 8-inch field howitzer be developed, with a carriage interchangeable with that preferred for the 155 mm gun. The howitzer was to have a range of not less than 16,000 yards.

With these criteria in mind, development of a replacement for the GPF began in 1920. At that time, the length of the barrel was increased, raising the range to 25,000 yards, an increase of 5,000 yards. The new weapons were designated M1920E and M1920M1E. However, a shortage of post–World War I funding meant that these weapons did not advance beyond the experimental stage.

Efforts to field an improved 155 were renewed in 1929, resulting in the 155 mm gun T4 on the T2 carriage, four examples of which were produced. This weapon had a longer barrel, a larger powder chamber, a redesigned breech, and a modernized firing mechanism, as compared to the M1918M1. The main gun tube was cold-worked, beginning with an inside diameter slightly less than the finished caliber. This manufacturing process, known as the container method, subjected the barrel to interior pressures up to 100,000 pounds per square inch, exceeding the firing pressure, essentially proofing the barrel before the first round was fired. Sharing a common carriage with the T4 was an 8-inch howitzer, T3.

On August 25, 1938, the T4 was standardized as the 155 mm gun M1. Although standardized, production of the M1 did not begin until October 1940. However, efforts to improve the weapon did not end there. Rather, on February 8, 1941, the improved M1A1 was standardized. The M1A1 differed from its predecessor by having the breech threads cut directly into the breech ring, eliminating the previously used breech bushing.

Further changes to the breech ring, driven by a number of breech ring failures at various army proving grounds, resulted in the M2, which was recommended for standardization on November 7, 1944, with final approval on March 15, 1945.

To provide mobility for the weapon, initially the M1 carriage was utilized both on the M1 and M1A1 guns. This was developed from the 155 mm gun–8-inch howitzer carriage T2, which had been tested by the Field Artillery Board in 1933 and was originally designed for the 8-inch howitzer M1920 and M1920M1E1. The designation was changed to M1 when Timken bogies were installed along with the 155 mm gun recoil mechanism M3. The bogie had four sets of dual 11.00-20 pneumatic tires mounted on two axles. The axles were connected by two upper and two lower torque rods assembled to the respective axles. When the bogie wheels were raised, the bottom carriage rested on the ground, which when combined with the spread trails provided three-point support for the weapon. The carriage was equipped with air brakes, controlled by the driver of the prime mover. Handbrakes were provided for the two front bogie wheels. T2 carriages, when brought up to M1 standard, were designated M1A1.

For travel, the gun was disconnected from the recoil mechanism by removing the piston rod nuts and was then retracted until the weight of the breech was supported by the travel lock. When being prepared for firing, the gun was pulled into battery by the prime mover. After the gun had been pulled into battery, the piston rods were reinstalled and the travel lock was removed. If the weapon was being towed by a Mack NO, a Mack coupler was used to support the trails, and the limber was not needed. A hoist on the truck would lower the trails when disconnected from the coupler.

If the weapon was being towed by a tractor, during transport the trails were supported by a limber. Initially, this was the M2 heavy carriage limber, adopted as standard in December 1939. The M2 was designed for high speed, with pneumatic tires and fifth-wheel steering. That is, the supported gun trails pivot on a fifth wheel, unlike earlier carriages, which locked the trails rigidly in place, and steering was accomplished by king pins, like the front axle of a truck. An A-frame design, the M3 limber was fitted with tires and wheels of the same size as those used on the carriage. A screw mechanism on the limber was used to lower the trails to the ground when emplacing the gun, and then the limber was removed.

In September 1943, the Bucyrus-Erie Company began development of the heavy carriage limber T8. More robust but also of a simplified design, this limber entered production and was standardized as the M5 in March 1944, by OCM 23188. The M5 had a straight axle with an arc that acted as a fulcrum, over which a cable was placed to lift the trails. This performed the function of the screw mechanism of the M2. Production of the M2 and M2A1 limbers had been terminated on January 1, 1944, in favor of the M5, and the older models were reclassified as limited standard. The M5 limber was also used by the M23 8-ton ammunition trailer.

While work on the 155 progressed rapidly, as seen, the howitzer version moved somewhat slower. The T3 was standardized as the 8-inch howitzer M1 in 1940 and entered production two years later, in July 1942. The howitzer and the gun had much in common and appear almost identical but for the length of the barrel. However, the recoil systems were set up differently, so converting from gun to howitzer or vice versa was a depot-level maintenance function.

In the 1920s, the US Army began developing a replacement for the French 155 mm GPF gun, which the Americans used in World War I and continued to use, in the form of the 155 mm gun M1918, in large numbers until the early part of World War II. This development work resulted in 1929 in the 155 mm gun T4 on carriage T2. This new gun had a maximum effective range of 25,000 yards, an almost 5,000-yard advantage over the 155 mm GPF. The 155 mm gun T4 on carriage T2 was given "substitute standard" status as the 155 mm gun M1 on carriage M1 on August 25, 1938. The M1 used a bushing between the barrel and the breech ring; subsequently, the 155 mm gun M1A1 was developed, on which the breech ring was screwed and shrunk directly onto the barrel. The 155 mm gun M1A1 was formally declared "standard" in June 1941. These guns, nicknamed "Long Toms," would prove their worth repeatedly during World War II and beyond. An early example of a 155 mm gun M1 is shown at Aberdeen Proving Ground, Maryland, during tests on December 23, 1940. Extra fixtures for test purposes were attached to the barrel and the gun cradle.

The 155 mm gun M1 on carriage M1 under evaluation at Aberdeen Proving Ground on September 23, 1940, is shown with the gun fully elevated, at +63 degrees, 20 minutes, and at full right traverse. The piece could be traversed 30 degrees to each side of center.

The following sequence of photos shows tests of a method of loading a 155 mm gun M1 into a 50-foot, double-door boxcar, at Rock Island Arsenal, Illinois, on September 11, 1940. Here, the gun is viewed from the rear, with the heavy carriage limber M2 in the foreground. *Rock Island Arsenal Museum*

The heavy carriage limber M2 was used early on with the 155 mm gun M1, supporting the rear of the trail during transport. The screw jack on the limber raised the trail to travel position; the top of the jack has a canvas cover over it, with the handles protruding from the cover. *Rock Island Arsenal Museum*

The carriage M1 on which the 155 mm gun M1 rested traveled on bogies with two sets of dual wheels per side. The rear left wheels are viewed through the open boxcar door. At the upper right are the traversing handwheel and the elevating arc or quadrant. *Rock Island Arsenal Museum*

More of the left side of the 155 mm gun M1 loaded in the boxcar is shown, including both left dual wheels, the forward end of the left trail, and, above the traversing handwheel, the left trunnion. The angled, telescoping cylinders are the left equilibrator. *Rock Island Arsenal Museum*

The right dual wheels are shown with wooden chocks installed in the boxcar. The wheels on the carriage M1 of the 155 mm gun M1 were attached to a two-axle bogie assembly that acted to lower the front of the carriage to the ground when placed in the firing position. *Rock Island Arsenal Museum*

The bogie assembly and dual wheels of the carriage M1 of the 155 mm gun M1 are seen from the front in this final photo of the boxcar-loading test at Rock Island Arsenal. In view are the hand brake levers, brake diaphragms, torque rods, front axle, and springs. *Rock Island Arsenal Museum*

Early on, various prime movers were tested with the 155 mm gun M1. In this 1941 photo, an International Harvester heavy tractor TD18 towing a 155 mm gun is under evaluation for the Field Artillery Board at Fort Bragg, North Carolina. The tractor carried eight men. *Rock Island Arsenal Museum*

In a March 19, 1941, photo at Rock Island Arsenal, the barrel of a 155 mm gun M1 has been hauled back to its travel position. The breech rests on a travel lock, and covers are on the gun from the front of the cradle assembly to the rear of the breech ring. *Rock Island Arsenal Museum*

In a companion photo to the preceding one, the canvas cover on a 155 mm gun M1 is viewed from the left front of the piece. Webbing straps to secure the front of the cover are attached by D rings to the cover and are secured and tightened by the use of buckles. *Rock Island Arsenal Museum*

The covers for the 155 mm gun M1 are viewed from the left side in a November 17, 1941, photo at Rock Island Arsenal. The cover for the breech ring seen in the first photo of this series is not installed. Also in view is the cable-and-turnbuckle tightener for the travel lock. *Rock Island Arsenal Museum*

The main cover for the gun was called the overall cover. During preparations for firing, under supervision of the ammunition corporal, crewmen numbers 9 to 12 would remove this cover and place it near the right bogie wheels. Number 9 would remove the breech cover. *Rock Island Arsenal Museum*

The overall cover is viewed from the right rear of the breech. On the right side of the breech is the breech-operating lever. On the rear of the breech is the breech-block carrier assembly, which provided the means for the interrupted-screw breechblock to swing open. *Rock Island Arsenal Museum*

During tests of the 155 mm gun M1 and carriage M1 at Aberdeen Proving Ground on December 11, 1940, the wheels of the heavy carriage limber M2 have sunk 8 inches into the mud. The upward-tilted handles of the screw jack are for lifting the trails to the limber. *Rock Island Arsenal Museum*

When the Army determined that the manual screw-jack operation of the heavy carriage limber M2 took too much time to raise and lower the trails of the 155 mm gun M1, a new limber was developed. As shown here on a 155 mm gun M1 and carriage M1, this limber was designated the heavy carriage limber M5. This limber depended on the winch of the gun's prime mover to operate a sling and a lift bracket on the limber axle, instead of a screw jack, to lift the trail to or remove it from the limber. The heavy carriage limber M5 took great care to operate properly.

A 155 mm gun M1 or M1A1 is secured to a railroad flatcar for transport. On the side of the left trail is the symbol for Battery C, 36th Field Artillery Regiment. In the foreground is what appears to be a limber, although it is neither the heavy carriage limber M2 nor M5.

A 155 mm gun M1 or M1A1 is in firing position. The front spades are stored on the sides of the trails; the rear spades were stored on the insides of the trails but are absent here. The trails were attached to the bottom carriage, which supported the top carriage and gun.

In parallel with the US Army's development of the 155 mm gun T4 on carriage T2 starting in the late 1920s, the Army also worked on the new 8-inch howitzer T3, using the same carriage T2 as the 155 mm gun, as seen here at Rock Island Arsenal, Rock Island, Illinois, on March 20, 1931. This howitzer featured a forged, auto-frettaged barrel and an Asbury breech mechanism of the same type found on the 155 mm gun. *National Archives*

The same 8-inch howitzer T3 on carriage T2 seen in the preceding photograph is viewed from the rear, with trails extended and howitzer tube at maximum elevation, at Rock Island Arsenal, on March 20, 1931. The arsenal was proud of the fact that its engineers had designed the carriage T2 in eighty-one days, and its staff had built the carriage in eighty-seven days. *National Archives*

A 10-ton tractor tows an 8-inch howitzer M3 on a carriage T2 at Aberdeen Proving Ground on May 23, 1931. *US Army Ordnance Museum*

An 8-inch howitzer T3 on a carriage T2 is shown in position before firing its first round during testing at Aberdeen Proving Ground, on July 28, 1931. A temporary frame, for test purposes, is attached to the gun cradle. Spare tires are on holders on the sides of the trail. *US Army Ordnance Museum*

The positions of the spades and the trails after firing one round are documented in this photo of the same 8-inch howitzer shown in the preceding photo, on the same date. On the side of the trail is a bracket into which the detachable spare-tire holder slid when in use. *US Army Ordnance Museum*

An 8-inch howitzer M1 on carriage M1 is viewed in a shop setting. The bottom carriage, visible below the front axle, has been lowered to the floor. This was accomplished by turning two bogie-lifting screws with large wrenches, lifting the wheels off the ground. *US Army Ordnance Museum*

Civilian workers at Aberdeen Proving Ground load an 8-inch howitzer during tests on December 1, 1941. By now the 8-inch howitzer T3 on carriage T2 had been standardized as the 8-inch howitzer M1 on carriage M1. Pettibone-Mullican Co. built this piece, no. 231. *US Army Ordnance Museum*

Weapon	155 mm gun	8-inch howitzer
Cannon model	M1A1	M1
Carriage model	M1	M1
Recoil mechanism	M3	M3
Production	1,882	1,006
Weight (lbs.)	40,000	31,600
Length (ft.)	40	34.3
Length of bore (caliber)	45	25
Max. elevation	65 degrees	64 degrees
Max. powder pressure	38,000 psi	33,000 psi
Rate of fire	1 round per minute	1 round per minute
Max. range (yds.)	25,395	18,510
Breech type	interrupted screw	interrupted screw
Ammunition	M101	M106
Ammo type	separate loading	separate loading
Projectile weight (lbs.)	94.7	200
HE fill (lbs.)	15.1	29.6
Propellant weight (lbs.)	32.2	107.5

In a photo dated April 11, 1945, an 8-inch howitzer M1 on carriage M1 is viewed from the front, providing clear details of the bogie assembly. A tow pintle is mounted on the center of the front axle. The muzzle of the howitzer is taped over for protection.

A private collector in England preserves this 155 mm gun, seen here coupled to a Mack NO 7½-ton 6 × 6 truck. Seen from this vantage point are the hand brake levers and the tow pintle on the front of the bogie assembly, as well as the front end of the model M3A1 recoil mechanism and the two equilibrators, to the sides of the gun tube. *John Blackman*

The 155 mm gun is retracted for travel, with the bottom of its breech secured to the triangular travel lock on the tops of the trails. The light-colored piece of equipment stored on brackets on the side of the trail is one of two front spades, which were attached to the front part of the carriage when emplacing the piece. *John Blackman*

The Mack NO prime mover bears registration number 548343 as well as replica markings for the 43rd Field Artillery, 5th Army. Above the open cab is a ring mount supporting a .50-caliber M2 HB machine gun. *John Blackman*

Replica markings for the tenth vehicle in the line of march and for Company B are on the left side of the bumper of a Mack NO. The nickname "FLOOZY" is painted in red and white on the front of the hood. Here, the canvas top has been installed over the cab. *John Blackman*

Battleship Memorial Park, Mobile, Alabama, preserves a 155 mm Long Tom, seen here with the battleship *Alabama* in the background. The bore of the muzzle has been permanently plugged. *Chris Hughes*

The 155 mm gun is set at approximately 23 degrees of elevation; maximum elevation was 63 degrees. The rear spades are installed on the trails of the carriage. *Chris Hughes*

Resting on the slab to the rear of the 155 mm gun at Battleship Memorial Park are the travel lock, a triangular-shaped weldment, and a heavy carriage limber M2, which formed the connection between the carriage of the 155 mm gun and its prime mover. *Chris Hughes*

The 155 mm gun and the limber are viewed from the rear. To the lower left of the top carriage (the part of the carriage the cradle rests on) is the traversing handwheel; the elevating handwheel is on the right side of the top carriage. The curved bar on the rear of the bogie is the arch axle; to the front of it is the carriage lock, which, preparatory to traveling, is swung upright and pinned to the two lugs on the bottom of the forward part of the cradle. *Chris Hughes*

Details of the front of the recoil mechanism, the top carriage, and the bogie are in view. The front part of the elevating sector (or elevating arc) is on the bottom of the cradle; a pinion acted with it to elevate the gun. Equipped with four dual wheels, the bogie supported the cradle end of the 155 mm gun during travel. *Chris Hughes*

The four sets of dual wheels and tires and parts of the springs and torque rods of the bogie are displayed. The tires were size 11.00-20; both the tires and the wheels were interchangeable with the heavy carriage limbers. *Chris Hughes*

The top of the bogie assembly is seen from the right side. The cylinders with spiral threads, topped with hexagonal caps, on each side of the carriage lock are bogie-lifting screws. When the gun was placed into battery, crewmen attached ratchet wrenches to the hex caps on the lifting screws; the turning of the screws lowered the carriage to the ground. The process was reversed to raise the carriage for travel. *David Doyle*

The hand brake levers, leaf springs and torque rods, bogie-lifting screws, and arch axle are observed from the side of the bogie. *Chris Hughes*

Faded but still intact 11.00-20 tires by multiple makers are mounted on the disc-and-rim wheels of the bogie assembly. *Chris Hughes*

In a view of the left side of the 155 mm gun, cradle, and upper carriage, the two separate cylinders with pipes attached to them along the forward part of the cradle are, *top*, the variable recoil housing and, *bottom*, the replenisher for the recoil system. Above them is the left equilibrator; the two equilibrators acted to balance the weight of the gun and cradle to the front of the trunnions and made elevating the piece at low elevations easier. *Chris Hughes*

On the left side of the upper carriage, below the panoramic telescope mount, is the traversing handwheel (*right*). The shaft from the wheel is connected to the traversing gearbox, *left*. Toward the top is the carrying case for the panoramic telescope. *David Doyle*

The left equilibrator and the left sides of the cradle and the upper carriage are viewed from the front. Projecting from the upper carriage to the right is the telescope mount M18A1, on which the panoramic telescope M12 would be mounted prior to firing. The panoramic telescope was used for laying the gun for indirect fire, when the target is not in view. The knurled cross-leveling knob is on the bottom of the mount. *David Doyle*

The rears of the equilibrators and the mount for the panoramic telescope are seen from the left side of the 155 mm gun. *Chris Hughes*

Atop the breech is a cylinder; this is the counterbalance, which is connected to the breechblock. The counterbalance allows the breechblock to be opened and closed with ease, and it holds the breechblock fully open during loading of the piece. *Chris Hughes*

Toward the lower right, on the side of the right trunnion, is a bracket, the quadrant mount M1, on which the gunner's quadrant, for laying the gun in elevation, was installed preparatory to firing the piece. To the left is the breech-operating handle. *Chris Hughes*

The off-center location of the counterbalance is shown in a photo of the rear of the 155 mm gun. The breechblock is attached to the breechblock carrier assembly, which acts as a hinge for the block. On the right side of the carrier is the breech-operating handle. Below the breech, on the left side of the rear of the cradle, is the rear of the recoil piston assembly. *Chris Hughes*

A limber, thought to be a heavy carriage limber M2, is displayed with the 155 mm gun at Battleship Memorial Park, Mobile, Alabama. The unit served as the link between the spade end of the trails of the gun carriage and the tow pintle of the prime mover. Its principal parts are an A-shaped drawbar; a suspension consisting of an axle, leaf springs, and two wheels with pneumatic tires; and a limber base and lifting mechanism mounted on the axle. *Chris Hughes*

The drawbar is equipped with a prop, which is lowered. The lunette on the front of the drawbar is resting on the travel lock of the 155 mm gun. *Chris Hughes*

When the 155 mm gun was coupled to the limber, the rears of the trails were attached to the bottom of the round plate: the limber base. Turning the four handles on the shaft above the limber base raised and lowered the trails. *Chris Hughes*

The limber is observed from the right rear, showing the four handles for operating the limber base. U-bolts secure the leaf springs to the axle. On top of the right side of the axle is a lock for the limber-lifting mechanism. For traveling, the lock was raised and engaged with one of the lift handles, to immobilize the lift. *Chris Hughes*

The heavy carriage limber M2 is viewed from the rear, showing further details of the lift lock, the axle, and the limber base. At the bottom of the screw of the lifting mechanism, under the limber base, is a block with pins that engaged bearings on the trails when the gun carriage was coupled to the limber. *David Doyle*

The same limber is observed from the right side. *Chris Hughes*

Details of the limber are viewed from above the drawbar. On the center of the tubular cross-member of the drawbar is a pin for locking the drawbar to the limber when the gun carriage is not coupled to the limber. *David Doyle*

Two bearings with pins that further secured the trails to the limber are on the underside of the limber. *David Doyle*

This 155 mm gun was photographed at the US Army Ordnance Museum at Aberdeen, Maryland. The gun tube is retracted to the travel position and is secured in the travel lock. *David Doyle*

The travel lock was constructed of welded steel and rested atop the trails during travel. Grab handles were provided for removing or installing it. The top of the lock pinned to a lug on the bottom of the breech. *David Doyle*

A wire-rope stay is fastened to the upper front of the travel lock, for extra bracing. *David Doyle*

From top to bottom: the rear of the recoil mechanism, the elevating arc, and the bottom carriage, to which the front of the stay for the travel lock is pinned. *David Doyle*

The trails of the 155 mm gun at the Ordnance Museum are secured to a heavy carriage limber M5. On this type of limber, a clamping bracket served to secure the trails; it is in the foreground in this photo. The steel cable to the right is the lifting sling, used in lifting the trails onto the limber. *David Doyle*

The clamping bracket, seen from the left side, was sandwiched between the rear ends of the trails and was secured with pins and bolts. *David Doyle*

The clamping bracket of the heavy carriage limber M5 is seen from the left front, with four grab handles welded to the claws on the top. To the lower right is the drawbar of the limber. *David Doyle*

Prominent in this view is the coupling pin of the limber, which is locked in place with a smaller pin furnished with a retainer chain. The curved object bolted to the axle to the lower right is the guide for the lifting sling. *David Doyle*

The bogie unit of the 155 mm gun at the Ordnance Museum is observed from above, with the hand brakes to the lower corners. The hexagonal tops of the bogie-lifting screws are fitted with a lock, to keep them from moving during travel. The carriage lock is pinned to the lugs on the bottom of the recoil mechanism. *David Doyle*

The carriage lock and the L-shaped locking pin with retainer chain are seen from the rear. *David Doyle*

In a display of a 155 mm gun and a heavy carriage limber M5 at the Texas Military Forces Museum, Camp Mabry, Austin, Texas, the clamping bracket is lying on the axle of the limber, revealing some details of the underside of the bracket. *Chris Hughes*

The center parts of the trails of the 155 mm gun at Camp Mabry are viewed from the right. Stored on brackets on the inside of the left trail are sections of the rammer staff, consisting of highly weathered wood with metal connections on the ends. To the upper right, the two rear spades are stored on the inside of the trails, and a front spade is on the outside of the left trail. Atop the trails to the rear of the webbing strap are brackets for the travel lock. *Chris Hughes*

Further details of the trails and stored spades are depicted, as well as the junctions of the trails with the lower carriage. The claw-shaped brackets on the rear of the lower carriage were for installing a trail brace, used when the piece was mounted on a firing platform. *Chris Hughes*

The US Army Field Artillery Museum, Fort Sill, Oklahoma, preserves this well-maintained 155 mm gun M1 on outdoor display. The front spades are stored on the trails, and the rear spades are installed at the rears of the trails. *John Charvat*

The gun, cradle, upper and lower carriages, and parts of the trails are in view. The mount for the quadrant is not installed on the side of the trunnion bearing. The pipe below the elevating handwheel is the elevating-mechanism clutch lever. *John Charvat*

The mount for the panoramic telescope is not included on the left trunnion bearing. The device on the left side of the breechblock carrier is the firing mechanism. An air filter for the compressed-air lines for the bogie brakes is on the forward end of each trail; the right one, to the far right of the photo. *John Charvat*

The right front spade is on its storage brackets on the right spade. To the rear of the spade on the side of the trail is a hex-shaped bracket for storing the ratchet end of a wrench operating the bogie-lifting screws. One of these wrenches was stowed on the outer side of each trail. *John Charvat*

The right rear spade is viewed from the rear, as installed on the spade. *John Charvat*

On the inner side of the left trail are four brackets for storing the left rear spade. On the outer side of the trail is stored the front left spade. Atop the trail to the rear of the spade is a bracket for the travel lock. *John Charvat*

Elements of the left side of the 155 mm gun, cradle and recoil system, equilibrators, carriage, and bogie are viewed from the side. The travel lock is engaged to the cradle. *John Charvat*

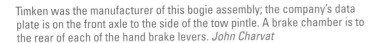

Timken was the manufacturer of this bogie assembly; the company's data plate is on the front axle to the side of the tow pintle. A brake chamber is to the rear of each of the hand brake levers. *John Charvat*

The bogie assembly is viewed from a different perspective. The bogie lifting screws are to the sides of the travel lock. *John Charvat*

This 8-inch howitzer M1 on carriage M1 is on display at the US Army Field Artillery Museum, Fort Sill, Oklahoma. As is the case with the museum's 155 mm gun M1, the panoramic-telescope mount is not installed on the trunnion cap. *John Charvat*

Supporting the rear of the 8-inch howitzer at Fort Sill is a heavy carriage limber M5. *John Charvat*

A view of the piece from the left rear shows the clamping bracket of the M5 limber, attached to the rears of the trails. To the lower rear of the clamping bracket is the curved guide for the lifting sling. *John Charvat*

On the end of the A-frame drawbar of the heavy carriage limber M5 is a steel block, which serves as the mount for the lunette: the ring that is secured to the tow pintle of the prime mover. Behind the center of the axle, the groove of the lifting-sling guide is in view. Jacks are supporting the axle. *John Charvat*

The clamping bracket for the limber is observed close-up, with the sling guide below. The horizontal pin with a tapering end that is inserted through the clamping bracket is the trail-coupling pin. The horizontal lock pin for the trail-coupling pin has been permanently welded in place. *John Charvat*

The clamping bracket is seen from the rear, with the tops of the trails of the 8-inch howitzer M1 in the background. The tapered end of the trail-coupling pin, along with its locking pin, is visible. *John Charvat*

In a view of the left side of the M5 limber, the drawbar is to the lower left. The structure from the trail-coupling pin down to the top of the axle is the limber-lifting bracket, which acted as a seat for the rear ends of the trails. To mount the trails of the howitzer on the limber, the trail-clamping bracket was bolted to the trail ends; that bracket was pinned to the limber-lifting bracket, and the trails were lifted to sit on the limber-lifting bracket by the action of the lifting sling operating in the sling guide. *John Charvat*

The left wheel and tire of the heavy carriage limber at Fort Sill are viewed from the side. *John Charvat*

The collections of the 45th Infantry Division Museum, Oklahoma City, Oklahoma, includes an 8-inch howitzer M1 on carriage M1. Shown here stored on the right trail are front and rear spades, and a travel-lock mounting bracket. *John Charvat*

The trails of an 8-inch howitzer photographed at the US Army Ordnance Museum, Aberdeen, Maryland, are in the travel position, with front and rear spades stored on them. At the lower center of the photo, on the outer side of the left trail, is a hex-shaped bracket for a wrench for the bogie-lifting screws. *John Charvat*

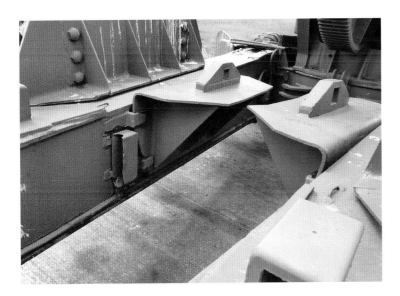

The two rear spades, for installation on the ends of the trails, are viewed close-up, along with part of a front spade, which was installed on the lower carriage prior to firing the piece. *John Charvat*

In a view of the left forward part of the cradle of the 8-inch howitzer at Aberdeen, the two cylinders below the front end of the left equilibrator are, *top*, the variable recoil housing and, *bottom*, the replenisher for the recoil system. Below is the bogie assembly. To the lower right are the traversing gearbox and traversing arc. *John Charvat*

The bogie assembly is seen from the right side of the howitzer cradle, including the arch axle, travel lock, two of the brake chambers, and hand brake levers. *John Charvat*

The front of the recoil mechanism on the howitzer cradle, as well as details of the bogie, is displayed. *John Charvat*

CHAPTER 2

Towing and Supplying the Cannons

The 155, which came to be known as the Long Tom, was initially towed by low-speed crawler tractors. The Mack NO, a 7½-ton 6 × 6 prime mover, was created to provide higher-speed travel for the gun and its crew. The NO was developed by Mack to provide a solution to a problem that Mack personnel had noticed while observing the Louisiana Maneuvers. Mack personnel were present because of the use of the 6-ton NM prime mover in conjunction with 3-inch antiaircraft guns.

Mack field service personnel noted the slow movement of large field artillery, including notably the 155 mm gun, when towed by slow-speed, fully tracked vehicles.

Mack proposed instead to use wheeled prime movers, and a hasty test utilizing a 6-ton NM coupled to a 155 mm GPF proved the merit of this concept but indicated the need for a larger truck.

Mack engineers soon, however, ran afoul of Army tradition. The Field Artillery branch believed that the weight of a wheeled prime mover should be twice that of the artillery piece it is intended to tow. The 155 mm gun weighed 31,000 pounds, and as a result, by the artillery branch's standards the prime mover should weigh 62,000 pounds. With these criteria, the gun and prime mover would weigh 93,000 pounds, a mass in excess of Corps of Engineers standards for bridges.

Mack had proposed eliminating the limber, which would place part of the weight of the towed load on the prime mover, thereby increasing traction and negating the artillery branch's reasoning for the high weight requirement for the prime mover. A hoist at the rear of the truck body was used to lift the trails so the Mack coupler could be used. This allowed a conventional cargo body to be used, thereby providing a place for the gun's crew, spare parts, or ammunition. After testing in 1941 the design was approved, and production of the new truck, model NO-2, began in January 1942. Successive models—the NO-3, NO-6, and NO-7—remained in production through June 1945.

In March 1944, the Allis-Chalmers M4 high-speed tractor entered production to provide relatively high-speed road travel as well as excellent off-road mobility. The M4 was initially produced in two configurations, depending on their intended purpose. Those with class A loads had ammunition stowage for 90 mm or 3-inch antiaircraft ammunition, while the class B loads were set up for 155 mm, 240 mm, or 8-inch ammunition. The ammunition stowage was at the rear of the vehicle, behind a cab that could accommodate the gun crew. A crane was provided for handling the class B ammunition. At the rear of the vehicle, beneath the ammunition door, was a 30,000-pound-capacity, PTO-driven winch that was used when placing the piece.

Field trouble, as a result of high ground pressure, brought about the June 1945 introduction of the M4A1, which had duckbill end connectors on the track, providing greater surface contact area and improved flotation. This required spacers to shift the suspension units away from the hull. Production of the M4-series tractors totaled 1,644 in 1943, 2,911 in 1944, and 1,256 in 1945. On August 14, 1945, all outstanding orders for further production of these tractors were terminated, canceling a further 3,661 of the vehicles.

In 1954, a rebuild program was initiated through contractor Bowen-McLauglin, which resulted in the M4A2 series of tractors.

In the years following World War II, the US Army began procuring a new generation of tactical wheeled vehicles, replacing the World War II–era designs across the board. The new designs drew on the lessons learned during World War II, and featured far-greater interchangeability of parts, improved performance, improved fording ability, and 24-volt electrical systems and were generally more robust. Replacing the NO in this new generation of vehicles was another Mack product, the M125 10-ton prime mover. While the NO was a formidable truck, the M125 was notably larger and was powered by a massive Le Roi TH-844 V-8 engine. The M125 was in production in 1957–58, and only a modest 552 units were built, reflecting the Army's increasing reliance on track-laying vehicles for artillery.

The M10 ammunition trailer (G-660, in the standard nomenclature of the War Department), was an important part of 155 mm gun and 8-inch howitzer batteries. Towed by prime movers, these trailers hauled ammunition for the big artillery pieces. They were fabricated from welded steel and ran on two tires, size 9.00-20. The M10 ammunition trailer weighed 2,090 pounds empty, and 4,848 pounds fully loaded. *Rock Island Arsenal Museum*

On the front of the A-type drawbar of the M10 ammunition trailer was a lunette, designed to pivot around its mounting pin, to allow for tow pintles of different heights on the prime movers. Next to the fuse box on the drawbar are the parking-brake levers. *TACOM LCMC History Office*

The M10 ammunition trailer was equipped with a fold-down landing gear for supporting the front end of the trailer when it was not hitched to a vehicle. Bows are installed to support a canvas cover, with footman loops on the body to hold down the cover. *TACOM LCMC History Office*

The M10 ammunition trailer had an overall length of 152.5 inches and a width of 85.25 inches. It was equipped with hand-operated parking brakes only. The tires were mounted on six-hole, combat-rim wheels with eighteen bolts. There were six lug nuts. *TACOM LCMC History Office*

Faintly visible on the tailgate of this M10 ammunition trailer is its Army registration number, 0781441. Recessed taillights are to the sides of the tailgate. On the rear bumper are a tow pintle, a reflector, and a receptacle and flip cover for an electrical connection. *TACOM LCMC History Office*

The metal box mounted on the drawbar of the M10 ammunition trailer was for storing projectile fuses. The fuse box held not only the fuses, but also essential tools and service manuals pertaining to the trailer and the ammunition it carried. *TACOM LCMC History Office*

The cover is installed on the M10 ammunition trailer. This trailer, registration number 0781441, was manufactured by the Youngstown Steel Door Co., of Youngstown, Ohio, and was photographed for the Engineering Standards Vehicle Laboratory, Detroit, on April 25, 1944. *TACOM LCMC History Office*

The same trailer is viewed from above. On the floor was a series of recesses, to keep mounting bolt heads and footman loops below the level of the floor. Some loops were mounted singly, and some doubly, and were used with straps for securing ammunition loads. *TACOM LCMC History Office*

In a June 19, 1942, photo at Aberdeen Proving Ground, an M10 ammunition trailer is loaded with eighteen 155 mm projectiles with ring-type fuse plugs, and six three-tube bundles of propellant charges. Each three-tube bundle was secured on the ends with "cloverleaf" caps. *US Army Ordnance Museum*

Another type of trailer used for transporting 155 mm projectiles was the M21 4-ton, two-wheel ammunition trailer (G-213 in War Department nomenclature). This trailer had twice the capacity of the M10 ammunition trailer, having a net weight of 5,300 pounds and a maximum gross weight of 13,300 pounds. The trailer was 144 inches long by 98 inches wide, and it rode on two size 14.00-20 tires. The M21 could hold seventy-two rounds of 155 mm ammunition, including projectiles, propellant charges, fuses, and primers. The Trailer Company of America received the initial contract for these trailers, but they subcontracted the assembly to the Herman Body Co., St. Louis, Missouri. *TACOM LCMC History Office*

This M21 ammunition trailer, US Army Ordnance serial number 150, was photographed for the Ordnance Operation, Engineering Standards Vehicle Laboratory, Detroit, on October 13, 1944. The drawbar is supported by the landing gear, which has a metal disc wheel. *TACOM LCMC History Office*

An M21 ammunition trailer, Ordnance number 150, is observed from above. On the floor are plates with cupped recesses for holding the bases of projectiles. Leaning inside the trailer are six perforated top racks that acted as retainers for the tips of the projectiles. *TACOM LCMC History Office*

On the M21 ammunition trailer, there is a placard on each door, warning that (1) the ammunition load must be evenly distributed over the axles and (2) the trailer's rear prop must be installed when the trailer is disconnected from the prime mover. *TACOM LCMC History Office*

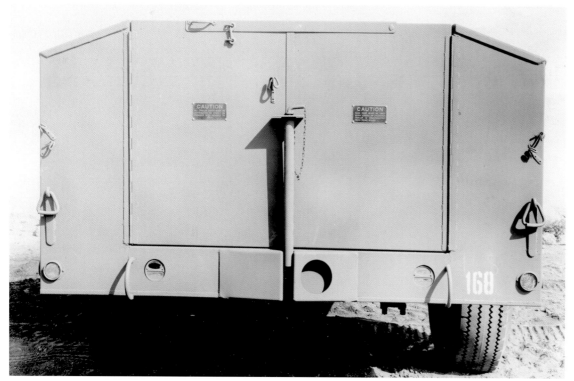

The tube between the rear doors of the M21 trailer is the rear prop. When in the travel position shown here, it acted as a doorstop. When the trailer was unhitched from its prime mover, the prop was lowered with its plate on the ground and secured with a pin. *TACOM LCMC History Office*

A third type of ammunition trailer used by 155 mm gun batteries was the M23 8-ton, four-wheel ammunition trailer (G-216), shown in a photo taken for the Ordnance Operation, Engineering Standards Vehicle Laboratory, Detroit, on March 12, 1945. This particular trailer was Ordnance number 233. The M23 was standardized in March 1945, and it could transport ammunition for 8-inch or 240 mm howitzers or the 155 mm gun. The trailer is shown configured for six-wheel operation with the mounting of a heavy carriage limber M5 at the front end, for tandem-trailer operation and to support up to 6,000 pounds of the gross load. Without the limber, the trailer could be connected directly to a 7½-ton prime-mover truck. *TACOM LCMC History Office*

The M23 ammunition trailer had a detachable crane for handling heavy ammunition, shown here hoisting a projectile by means of the ring-type fuse plug. The projectile is marked "8 H," indicating it is for an 8-inch howitzer. A tow pintle is mounted in a recess on the rear of the chassis. On the floor of the trailer are cup-shaped holders for the bases of projectiles.

An M23 ammunition trailer is viewed from above. Six hinged-top racks for projectiles are installed; the front and center racks are closed, but the two rear racks are swung open, revealing the stored projectiles. Also in view are the limber and the fuse box.

In a view dated October 23, 1944, an M23 ammunition trailer is seen from the front right. A well for a spare tire was on the right front of the trailer body. The fuse box was mounted on the front of the body. Fittings for air brake hoses are on the front of the trailer. A boom on the truck was necessary to lift the A-frame up to the pintle. *TACOM LCMC History Office*

An M23 ammunition trailer is loaded with ninety-six complete rounds of 155 mm gun ammunition. On the bottom are the projectiles. Stacked above the top projectile rack are propellant charges in three-round cloverleaf packs: thirty-two packs in total.

THE FIELD ARTILLERY BOARD
FORT BRAGG, N.C.

Neg. No. 136-1944	Date 7-4-1944
Exhibit C-1	File No. 451.3
Test No. 0-61-L	Item No. 735

Ammunition Trailer, 8 Ton, M23 Loaded with 96 complete rounds of 155mm Gun ammunition.

The M23 ammunition trailer had a load capacity of sixty complete rounds of 8-inch howitzer ammunition, as opposed to ninety-six rounds of 155 mm ammo. The cloverleaf packing tubes for the propellant charges are secured with webbing straps.

THE FIELD ARTILLERY BOARD
FORT BRAGG, N.C.

Neg. No. 136-1944	Date 7-4-1944
Exhibit D-1	File No. 451.3
Test No. O-61-L	Item No. 735

Ammunition Trailer, 8 Ton, M23 Loaded with 60 complete rounds of 8"howitzer ammunition.

This October 13, 1944, photo shows an M23 ammunition trailer, Ordnance number 235, with the front end resting on the landing gear, which was a swing-down unit with a small metal wheel. The method of lashing the canvas cover is illustrated.

The M23 ammunition trailer is viewed from the left rear. The Army registration number is faintly visible on the left door: 0800329. A heavy-duty lifting ring is on each upper corner of the rear of the trailer; similar rings are on the front corners of the trailer.

The rear doors, with their double-walled construction, are open on this M23 ammunition trailer, Ordnance number 233. On the floor, the cups that formed the bottom racks were in three different sizes, to fit the 155 mm gun, 8-inch howitzer, or 240 mm howitzer ammunition.

This November 1944 photo was taken to document a direct coupling, without a limber, between the A-frame of an M23 ammunition trailer and a swiveling pintle on the rear of a 7½-ton 6 × 6 truck. A boom on the rear of the truck was used to lift the trails to the pintle.

The Mack NO 7½-ton 6 × 6 trucks (War Department designation G-532) were one of several types of prime movers that towed the 155 mm guns and 8-inch howitzers. The NOs were intended as a stopgap prime mover for these artillery pieces until the M4 high-speed tractor came on line. The Mack 7½-ton 6 × 6 trucks could pull a maximum towed load of 50,000 pounds: well within the weights of the 155 mm gun M1 and 8-inch howitzer M1 and their carriages. The version of the Mack 7½-ton 6 × 6 shown here, model NO-6, was photographed at the Ordnance Operation, Studebaker Proving Ground, on June 29, 1944. A total of 1,000 NO-6s were completed, with deliveries in 1943 and 1944. These trucks were assigned Army registration numbers 544440 to 545439. *TACOM LCMC History Office*

The Mack NO-2 was the first production model of the Mack 7½-ton 6 × 6 prime mover, the NO-1 having been a one-off prototype. A total of 403 NO-2s were delivered. It had a winch behind the curved front bumper and a lifting arch and hoist at the rear. *Mack Historical Museum*

A Mack 7½-ton 6 × 6 with registration number 544677 is shown on May 2, 1944. These trucks had wooden bodies with stakes and open, military-style cabs. At the rear of the cargo body are the chain hoist and lifting arch and the stored bracket for hitching an artillery piece. *TACOM LCMC History Office*

The Mack 7½-ton 6 × 6 prime movers hauled not only the 155 mm guns and 8-inch howitzers, but also ammunition trailers. This photo taken for the Ordnance Operation, Engineering Standards Vehicle Laboratory, Detroit, on November 24, 1944, shows a 7½-ton 6 × 6 truck with an M23 8-ton, four-wheel ammunition trailer hitched to it. The air hoses for the trailer's air brakes were not connected on this occasion. The tarpaulin is installed over the cargo body, and a canvas top is secured over the cab. *TACOM LCMC History Office*

The lifting arch in the rear of the cargo body was removable, its legs being inserted in sockets in the floor. A chain hoist for lifting and lowering the trails of hitched artillery pieces was suspended from the arch. On the rear cross-member of the chassis frame was a universal coupler, attached to which (in this photo) is the bracket for attaching an artillery piece or ammunition trailer. Three staggered bent-rod steps were attached to each of the mud flaps. *Mack Historical Museum*

A Mack NO-6 7½-ton 6 × 6 prime mover is viewed from the right rear, with the universal coupler removed from the rear of the chassis frame. Crew seats were to the rears of the two spare tires in the cargo body. A recessed toolbox was located below the tailgate. *Mack Historical Museum*

A Mack NO-2, registration number 522497, is being loaded on a transporter. At the front end of the cargo body is a steel frame that served as a cab protector. A diagonal steel-rod brace is visible at each upper corner of the frame. The exhaust is behind the front mud flap. *Mack Historical Museum*

Manufactured by Allis-Chalmers, the M4 18-ton, high-speed tractor (G-150) was designed to meet the need for a powerful, fully tracked vehicle capable of towing a variety of artillery pieces. Some M4s designated as class A were for transporting 90 mm or 3-inch guns, crews, and ammunition. The class B tractors were designed for hauling 155 mm guns and 8-inch or 240 mm howitzers, crews, and ammunition, and they featured a crane for handling ammunition. Power was supplied by the Waukesha 145GZ six-cylinder engine, rated at 190 horsepower at 2,100 rpm; the maximum towed load was 38,700 pounds. Production of the M4 lasted from March 1943 to June 1945, with 5,552 examples being completed.

As seen in a photo of an M4 with registration number 970994 on September 27, 1944, the class B vehicles had a single steel plate on the sides of the rear of the body. On class A tractors, these plates had doors. To the fronts of those plates were engine-ventilation grilles.

An emplacing pintle was mounted under the front bumper of the M4. On the roof above the rear passenger compartment was a ring mount for a Browning M2 .50-caliber machine gun. Two spotlights were mounted on the front, with protective wire grilles.

A tailgate with a V-shaped strengthener was on the upper rear of the body of the M4 high-speed tractor. To the sides of the tailgate were rear spotlights. On the lower rear of the hull was a tow pintle and couplings for air hoses for the brakes of towed guns or trailers.

An M4 high-speed tractor with a class B ammunition compartment is viewed from above. The ammunition compartments are painted white. In the center compartment are top racks for securing projectiles. A crane is installed in the left rear of that compartment.

The M4A1 18-ton, high-speed tractor was similar to the M4, the main changes being the addition of duckbill extensions on each side of the track assemblies, bogies extended from the hull to compensate for the track extensions, and wider fenders and front bumper.

The M4A1 high-speed tractor, with its track extensions, is viewed from the rear. Above the top of the ammunition box are several tubes containing propellant charges, as well as the upper part of the ammunition-handling crane. Chains were provided for the tailgate.

As a modification on the M4A1s, two louvered plates were fastened to each side of the ammunition box, for ventilation. The cab doors were made of canvas and soft-plastic windows on frames; when open, the doors overlapped each other, as seen here.

In a left-rear view of an M4A1 high-speed tractor, the bottom of the support for the crane protrudes through the body to the lower left of the left door. The winch, driven by the power takeoff, was in the lower rear of the hull, visible through the oblong cutouts.

An M4A1 high-speed tractor is viewed from above with a full load of ammunition on July 27, 1945. In the center ammunition compartment are twelve projectiles, stored upright, with top racks installed. To the sides are twelve canisters with propellant charges, six per side.

An M4 high-speed tractor with an M23 ammunition trailer hitched to it is undergoing evaluations by the Field Artillery Board at Fort Bragg, North Carolina, on July 4, 1944. A tarpaulin is lashed over the trailer body, and air hoses for the trailer's brakes are installed.

During testing by the Ordnance Operation, Engineering Standards Vehicle Laboratory, Detroit, Michigan, on March 22, 1945, an M4 18-ton, high-speed tractor is towing an M23 18-ton, four-wheel ammunition trailer. Although the Mack NO 7½-ton trucks were able to draw loaded M23 trailers hitched directly to the trucks, when the M4 high-speed tractor hauled the fully loaded M23 trailer, it was necessary to use a limber, to distribute the weight. *TACOM LCMC History Office*

In 1957 and 1958, Mack produced the M125 10-ton trucks (G-792), with a total production run of 552 vehicles. The M125 was intended as a prime mover for 155 mm guns and 8-inch howitzers. Some of the components of the M125 were borrowed from the Mack NO 7½-ton trucks. The engine was the Le Roi T-H844, with 297 horsepower at 2,600 rpm. A winch driven by the power takeoff was mounted on the front end, rated at 45,000 pounds. Winch-cable rollers were mounted on the center of the front bumper. *TACOM LCMC History Office*

An M125 10-ton Army truck, registration number 5B1382, is viewed from above. Visible on top of the front-mounted winch are the level-wind assembly and swivel sheave, a trolley system that allowed for tightly winding rows and layers of cable on the winch. *Mack Historical Museum*

In a rear view of this M125 10-ton truck, registration number 5B1606, the davit, absent the associated chain hoist, for lifting and lowering the trails of artillery pieces during coupling and uncoupling operations is on the rear of the cargo body. *Mack Historical Museum*

On the rear cross-member of the chassis frame of the M125 is the yoke block for attaching a drawbar and trail clamp: a fixture attached to the trail of an artillery piece that served a purpose similar to a lunette. A tow pintle also could be interchanged with the yoke. *Mack Historical Museum*

A Mack M125 10-ton truck, registration number 5B1368, is loaded on a flatcar for long-distance transport. Visible above the front tire is a driveshaft and roller chain: part of the drive system for the front winch. The swivel sheave may be seen above the winch.

During World War II, the Long Tom was issued to forty-nine battalions, with forty battalions sent to Europe, beginning with Tunisia in 1943, while seven battalions were sent to the Pacific. Fifty-nine battalions using 8-inch howitzers were raised, with thirty-eight going to Europe and three to the Pacific.

Continuing its service beyond World War II, during the 1950s the Long Tom was redesignated the "155 gun M59," with the single nomenclature replacing the previously used lengthy "155 mm gun M1A1 with M1A1 carriage and M5 limber." Likewise, the 8-inch was also redesignated in the 1950s, first as the M115 8-inch howitzer and later as the M115 203 mm howitzer. The newly developed Mack M125 10-ton 6 × 6 prime mover replaced the previously used wheeled and tracked prime movers as the tow vehicle both for the howitzer and the cannon.

As the US military moved increasingly toward self-propelled artillery, the Long Tom and 8-inch howitzer were supplied to allied nations, some of which continued to use the weapons into the 1990s.

During field maneuvers by the Second Army in Tennessee in the early 1940s, a crawler tractor is towing a 155 mm gun M1A1 on a carriage M1 with a heavy carriage limber M2 attached. Following the towed artillery piece is a long column of crawler tractors, with at least the first one towing an artillery trailer. Slow-speed crawler tractors were often used in combat conditions to move the big guns and howitzers across difficult terrain.

A 155 mm gun M1A1 is being maneuvered through a forest by a crawler tractor, partially visible to the far right. The 155 mm gun barrel is retracted to its travel position, with the breech end supported by a substantial travel lock. Spare tires are mounted on the trails, as are the spades. Painted on the trail is the symbol of Battery C, 36th Field Artillery Regiment, featuring crossed cannons.

Spectators on a grandstand, part of the 5,000 attendees at the twentieth annual meeting of the Army Ordnance Association at Aberdeen Proving Ground, Maryland, watch as a 155 mm gun M1 passes by, towed by a crawler tractor, on October 12, 1939.

Twelve 155 mm guns M1 or M1A1 on carriages M1 are lined up at Fort Bragg, North Carolina, during a demonstration for Secretary of War Henry L. Stimson around May 1942. These guns were assigned to the Provisional Field Artillery Brigade.

During Second Army Maneuvers in Tennessee on November 5, 1942, two members of the crew of a 155 mm gun M1A1 from Battery A, 119th Field Artillery Regiment, are preparing to fire the piece. According to the original label of the photograph, this gun was a "1942 model." The artilleryman to the left is adjusting the panoramic telescope, while the one to the right has the firing lanyard pulled tight.

The 155 mm guns M1A1 began to arrive in England for the coming campaigns by November 1942, when this photo was taken of artillerymen cleaning the bore of their piece during field maneuvers. Ten soldiers are manning the bore-cleaning staff.

The crew seen in the preceding photo is viewed from another angle as they clean the bore of the 155 mm gun. These troops were from the 36th Field Artillery Regiment, and the site was at the British Army's training grounds at Salisbury Plain, November 1942.

In a continuation of the activities depicted in the preceding two photos, the 155 mm gun M1A1 has been loaded and now is elevated to a high angle. The crewmen are at their positions preparatory to firing. Worthy of mention is how the trail and the bottom carriage rested firmly on the ground when the piece was in firing position.

A Mack NO 7½-ton truck is towing a 155 mm gun M1A1 across a muddy field at an undisclosed location in early 1943. Covers are installed on the breech and the muzzle. This photograph was used to illustrate an article in *Coast Artillery Journal*. *Mack Historical Museum*

During an exercise, a Mack NO 7½-ton truck with an 8-inch howitzer M1 has paused in a sandy field. This M1 8-inch howitzer is on an M1 carriage but has distinctive coil-spring equilibrators of the type associated with the 155 mm howitzer M1. *Mack Historical Museum*

The same Mack NO and 8-inch howitzer M1 combination seen in the preceding photo is observed from a different perspective. When an artillery piece was directly coupled to the prime mover, it was referred to as a trailed load; a semitrailed load employed a limber. *Mack Historical Museum*

This is the final photo in a series of three depicting a Mack NO towing an 8-inch howitzer M1 around early 1943. Fastened to the rear ends of the trails is a clamp bracket; this bracket was in turn attached to a yoke on the NO truck to form the coupling.

A Mack NO 7½-ton truck is drawing a 155 mm gun M1A1 on a carriage M1 at Aberdeen Proving Ground in early 1943. This truck is equipped with stanchions for attaching a ring mount for a .50-caliber machine gun above the cab, for antiaircraft defense. *Mack Historical Museum*

Crewmen of a 155 mm gun M1A1 crouch and clasp their hands over their ears just after the no. 1 man of the crew, to the rear of the breech, has pulled the firing lanyard. A longer lanyard was available if the chief of section ordered no. 1 to stand outside the trails.

The crew of a 155 mm gun M1A1 have just fired the piece during a training exercise at Fort Sill, Oklahoma, home of the US Army Field Artillery School, in 1943. The artilleryman to the left is standing next to a water bucket and bore-cleaning brush.

This photo was taken a split second apart from the preceding photo, judging by the positions and attitudes of the crew members. To the far right, two crewmen are crouching by several loading trays holding 155 mm projectiles, ready for loading.

Two 155 mm guns M1A1 are on the firing line during a training exercise at Fort Sill, Oklahoma, around February 1943. The closest piece has just fired, and its barrel is in recoil. In the left background, two artillerymen are observing the effect of the fire.

During the training exercise at Fort Sill, the gunner has called "Ready," the section chief—to the rear of the trails with right hand raised— prepares to give the order to fire, and the no. 1, to the rear of the breech, stands ready to pull the lanyard to fire the piece.

In a small clearing in a dense thicket at Camp Gruber, Oklahoma, on April 28, 1943, PFC George Daniels, the no. 1 of the crew of a 155 mm gun M1A1 from Battery C, 137th Field Artillery Battalion, is prepared to pull the lanyard to fire the piece. The lanyard was attached to a trigger mechanism on the firing lock M17 mounted on the breechblock. Just visible at right is a tire and wheel of the limber.

In a photo taken on the same occasion as the preceding one, a 155 mm gun M1A1 of Battery C, 137th Field Artillery Battalion, has just fired. The nickname "CHERRY" is on the barrel, in keeping with the practice of nicknaming guns following the battery's letter.

The 155 mm guns M1 and M1A1 first saw combat in the North African Campaign. This example, hitched to a limber and a TD18 heavy tractor (G-101), was photographed at Oran, Algeria, on April 6, 1943. The muzzle of the 155 mm gun is taped over to keep out dust, moisture, and foreign objects. Above the breech and between the supports for the equilibrators is a vertical sheave on a bracket. This sheave was used in conjunction with a winch cable when retracting the barrel into travel position, or in moving the barrel forward into firing position.

The TD18 tractor seen in the preceding photo is viewed from the front. International Harvester produced these tractors from 1938 to 1957, completing approximately 22,000 at the IH plant at Melrose Park, Illinois. A Gar Wood winch was on the front end.

During the Tunisian Campaign of 1942–43, an International Harvester M1 heavy tractor with markings on the bumper for the 36th Field Artillery Regiment is towing a 155 mm gun M1A1 through a war-torn town. A heavy carriage limber M2 is employed.

A heavy tractor is towing a 155 mm gun M1A1 along a muddy trail on Rendova Island in New Georgia, Solomon Islands, on July 2, 1943, two days after the US invasion of that island. In conditions such as this, a heavy crawler tractor was virtually the only way to move heavy artillery. The trails of the gun are coupled to a heavy carriage limber M2; above the tires of the limber is the characteristic screw jack (with a cover over it) and four handles of the M2. Crates and equipment are stowed on the trails of the gun.

Marines of the 155 mm Group of the 9th Defense Battalion are emplacing one of their guns in a firing position in a clearing in a palm grove on Rendova on July 2, 1943. Stenciled in small letters on the barrel of the gun, near the muzzle, is "SNIPER."

On July 2, 1943, a 155 mm gun M1A1 of the 9th Defense Battalion is emplaced and ready to be fired at the Japanese-held airport 11 miles away at Munda, on Rendova Island. "SEMPER" and another word, undoubtedly "FIDELIS," is stenciled on the gun barrel.

In this general view of a battery of the Marines' 9th Defense Battalion preparatory to firing at Japanese forces at the Munda airport on July 21, 1943, in addition to the 155 mm gun M1A1 in the foreground, there are three more guns interspersed among the palms.

Camouflage netting has been rigged around the 155 mm gun M1A1 of the 9th Defense Battalion, nicknamed "SNIPER," seen in a previous photograph, shortly before the guns of that battalion began the bombardment of the Japanese-held airport at Munda.

A fighter plane is attacking a 155 mm gun M1A1 of the 190th Field Artillery during Field Problem Cannon, near Marlborough, England, on May 11, 1943. In certain scenarios in combat, usually no sooner was a gun emplaced than the crew erected camouflage netting.

Men of Battery C, 190th Field Artillery, serve a 155 mm gun during Field Problem Cannon, near Marlborough, England, on May 11, 1943. Both the 155 mm Long Tom and the 8-inch howitzer M1 had the cylinder on the upper right of the breech.

A tractor, hidden behind the building to the right, tows a 155 mm gun M1A1 around a street intersection in Campobello, Sicily, during the Allied invasion of that island, on July 13, 1943. A bunched-up camouflage net is secured to the top of the gun barrel.

A gun crew stands at the ready to fire a camouflaged 155 on the island of Kodiak, in the Aleutian Islands. The Aleutians was the site of the only successful invasion of North America during World War II.

Members of the 1st Battalion, 190th Field Artillery Regiment, based at Devizes, Wiltshire, England, are serving a 155 mm gun M1A1 during training in England on August 1, 1943. Two men are ramming a projectile, while the man to the left carries a propellant charge.

On August 1, 1943, a dozen 155 mm guns M1A1 of 1st Battalion, 190th Field Artillery, are on a firing line during a training session in England. The 190th Field Artillery was a Pennsylvania National Guard unit, redesignated 190th Field Artillery Group in November 1943.

During the same training session documented in the two preceding photos, the crew of a 155 mm gun M1A1 of 1st Battalion, 190th Field Artillery, sack out after firing practice. On the closest gun, a cloth cover has been placed over the equilibrator's telescoping joint.

A photographer snapped this view the instant a 155 mm gun M1A1 of 1st Battalion, 190th Field Artillery, was fired, during a field exercise in England, on August 1, 1943. Stacked rifles, camouflage netting, liquid containers, and the travel lock are in the foreground.

A US Army 155 mm gun M1A1 is being towed ashore from a landing craft at Caronia during Operation Husky, the invasion of Sicily, on August 3, 1943. The only covers are on the breech and the muzzle. The nickname "DOOM" has been painted on the side of the trail.

A 155 mm gun M1A1 from Battery B, 36th Field Artillery Regiment, is being towed inland from the beach at Caronia, Sicily, on August 3, 1943. The prime mover is a military 10-ton 6 × 6 wrecker with a rear winch. To the front is a crawler tractor.

A Mack NO 7½-ton truck is pulling a 155 mm gun M1A1 up a steep draw in Sicily on August 2, 1943. Unit markings on the rear of the Mack prime mover are faint, but "36F" for 36th Field Artillery Regiment is visible on the left side of the tailgate.

The following sequence of photos is a document of the emplacement of 155 mm artillery at a firing site in the Cerami area of north-central Sicily, on August 2, 1943. Here, preparations are underway to emplace the front spades and install the barrel-retraction cable.

Two crewmen atop a 155 mm gun M1A1 are rigging the cable by which the prime mover's winch will pull the gun barrel into battery position. The cable was attached to a ring on the barrel and routed around a sheave between the equilibrators, and thence to the winch.

By operating the big wrench, two crewmen are raising the bogie assembly, thus drawing the wheels off the ground and allowing the bottom carriage of the 155 mm gun to settle onto the ground. Each gun had two bogie wrenches, stored on the outer sides of the trails.

The artillerymen in the foreground are digging a pit for the rear spade of the right trail of a 155 mm gun M1A1 in the Cerami area of Sicily, on August 2, 1943. When not in use, the rear spades were stored on carriers on the inner sides of the trails.

In the Cerami area on August 2, 1943, the left rear spade of a 155 mm gun has been emplaced in a pit, and crewmen are securing the rear of the trail to the spade, using a key. The purpose of the spades was to keep the gun carriage from kicking free of its position.

One of the final steps in preparing a 155 mm gun M1A2 for firing was to erect a camouflage net over the piece. Several crewmen are in the process of rigging the net. The man in the center foreground is standing next to the travel lock for the breech end of the gun.

In the last of the series of photos of the emplacement of 155 mm guns in the Cerami area of Sicily, on August 2, 1943, Pvt. Nick Cucinotti of Philadelphia, Pennsylvania, has shimmied out to the front end of a 155 mm gun to kiss the barrel in appreciation.

Members of the 2/6th Field Regiment (Australian) are serving a well-camouflaged 155 mm gun M1A1 at the village of Buoisi during the Salamaua-Lae Campaign in New Guinea on September 11, 1943. Earlier in the war this unit had seen action in North Africa.

On September 20, 1943, a 155 mm gun M1A1 is part of Allied forces advancing to the south of Battipaglia, Italy. A heavy crawler tractor is towing the piece over a pontoon bridge. The nickname "HUN'S HORROR" is stenciled on the gun's recoil assembly.

A 155 mm gun M1A1 from Battery C, 36th Field Artillery, fires a round at German forces in the mountains near San Angelo, Italy, on October 23, 1943. The barrel is in full recoil. The gun was concealed in a stand of trees, providing some cover from enemy eyes.

The crew of a 155 mm gun of Battery C, 36th Field Artillery, prepare to fire the piece near San Angelo, Italy, on October 23. 1943. All wear the number 13 on their M1 helmets. Two hold a loading tray with a projectile while the two men to the right ram the projectile.

In another photo of the same 155 mm piece shown in the preceding photo, a projectile has been rammed into the chamber, and the no. 5 crewman is inserting a bagged propellant charge into the breech. To his right, no. 1 has his hand on the breech-operating lever.

At a revetted firing position in the Selvone area of Italy on January 10, 1944, two crewmen of a 155 mm Long Tom are preparing to manually turn the screw jack on a heavy carriage limber M2 in order to lower the trail of the piece to the ground.

A soldier is removing the hook from a 10-ton 6 × 6 wrecker, which has just lowered the tube of a 155 mm gun M1A1 onto its carriage. The work was performed by the 109th Medium Maintenance Ordnance Company in the Presenzano area of Italy on January 24, 1944.

Smoke is issuing from the muzzle of a just-fired 8-inch howitzer M1 of the 995th Field Artillery Battalion near Mignano, Italy, on January 1, 1944. The nickname "CONQUEROR" is stenciled on the barrel. In the center background is Monte Sammucro.

Members of the crew of a 155 mm gun M1A1 are sitting on the M4 high-speed tractor that is towing the piece, en route to a new position in the hills near Pozzilli, Italy, on January 11, 1944. A tarpaulin is secured to footman loops on the rear of the M4.

The no. 1 155 mm gun of Battery C, 173rd Field Artillery Battalion, was photographed between fire missions in the Rocchetta area of Italy on January 16, 1944. The gun was in a sandbagged emplacement, and camouflage nets weren't necessary because of the tree cover.

An M4 high-speed tractor, next to the pile of stones toward the right, is emplacing a 155 mm gun M1A1 at a firing position in the Pozzilli area in Italy on January 11, 1944. The gun bears the nickname "CRAPS" on the barrel near the muzzle, while the nickname "CALABOOSE" is stenciled on the side of the M4 tractor, an indication that the vehicle and the gun were assigned to a Battery C. The high-speed tractor is piled high with bedrolls, tents, and equipment, and four 5-gallon liquid containers are on the rear of the hull.

During the landings at Anzio, Italy, on February 13, 1944, a 155 mm gun M1A1 is disembarking from LST-430. An M4 18-ton, high-speed tractor is the prime mover for the gun. Uncharacteristically, this M4 is the class A type, which was designed to transport 90 mm guns, ammunition, and crews. This is distinguished by the horizontal joint on the middle of the rear side plate of the ammo compartment. On the bumper are markings for Battery C, 4th Battalion, 77th Field Artillery, 5th Army.

An M4 high-speed tractor is pulling a 155 mm gun M1A1 up a street in the Nettuno, Italy, area on February 13, 1944. The M4 is the class A version, as indicated by the short tailgate; class B, intended for 155 mm guns, had a tall tailgate with a "V" strengthener.

On February 15, 1944, four 155 mm guns M1A1 are stored in a field in England, for eventual use in the invasion of Normandy planned for that year. In the right background are heavy carriage limbers M2. In the center background are 40 mm Bofors guns.

A 155 mm gun M1A1 is in a firing position covered by a natural embankment in the Acquafondata area in Italy on February 12, 1944. This was in the French Corps area, and several men to the left are wearing French helmets. To the right is a limber.

Members of the 173rd Field Artillery Battalion load a projectile into a 155 mm gun in the Scapoli area of Italy on February 22, 1944. The gun is under camouflage netting. The gunner is crouching on the left trail, peering through the panoramic telescope.

On February 15, 1944, PFC George W. Spence of Battery F, 36th Field Artillery, loads a propellant charge into the breech of a 155 mm gun M1A1. The interrupted-screw design of the breechblock is illustrated. A loading tray was not necessary for inserting charges.

The no. 5 crewman of a 155 mm gun inserts a propellant charge into the piece, near Nettuno on February 13, 1944. The cylinder on the upper right of the breech ring was a mechanism to assist in closing the breech, which was difficult to do wholly by hand.

The African American crew of Section 2, Battery B, 49th Coast Artillery, serve a 155 mm gun M1A1 on Bougainville, in the northern Solomon Islands, on April 16, 1944. Two of the crewmen are ramming a projectile into the breech while two others hold the loading tray.

At a repair facility in the Anzio area on April 3, 1944, members of the 101st Medium Maintenance Ordnance Company are placing a 155 mm gun tube on a carriage M1. A 10-ton 6 × 6 wrecker is hoisting the tube, which weighed about 9,000 pounds, into place.

The ruins of an 8-inch howitzer M1 and its Mack NO prime mover were photographed on a street in Buonconvento, Italy, on July 1, 1944. The truck, which was loaded with 8-inch ammunition, had run over a land mine, setting off the ammunition. All the tires were burned off both vehicles. The twisted remains of the cab protector are visible to the rear of the truck cab.

The 155 mm Long Toms were key players in the Normandy invasion, such as this example that an M4 high-speed tractor with a class B ammunition box is towing through a French town in the Torigni sector of Normandy on July 30, 1944.

A Mack NO 7½-ton 6 × 6 truck is transporting a 155 mm gun M1A1 through a French resort town on August 14, 1944. What appears to be a section of metal fencing material is secured to the top of the gun tube to form a storage rack for camouflage netting.

On August 18, 1944, a Mack NO truck is hauling a 155 mm Long Tom along a hilly road toward Brest, France, where a battle had been raging for eleven days for the possession of that key port. The gun's crewmen are sitting on supplies stacked in the truck's cargo body.

French girls greet the crew of a 155 mm Long Tom on the road to Brest on August 18, 1944. The Mack NO prime mover's registration number, 544946, is visible on the tailgate. A large crate and other gear are stowed on the trails of the gun carriage.

Long Tom crewmen are sitting on the roof of an M4 high-speed tractor that is towing a 155 mm gun through Oiselay, France, on September 11, 1944. This gun was assigned to the 77th Field Artillery, 7th Army. The M4 was equipped with tracks with rubber shoes.

Painted on the tube of this 8-inch howitzer M1 near Rambervillers, France, on October 29, 1944, was "ADOLPH [sic], COUNT YOUR MEN / 2nd." The Mack NO prime mover had the name "ANGEL" on the door and was equipped with tire chains for better traction.

When the US Army returned to the Philippines in 1944, it brought its heavy artillery, including Long Toms. This 155 mm gun is in a prepared firing position outside Dulang, Leyte, Philippines, on October 18, 1944. The gun is being fired, since the crewmen are covering their ears with their hands. The nickname "Cecelia" is painted in script on the gun tube near the muzzle. Another Long Tom is in the right background.

Two 155 mm guns are in action outside Dulang on October 29, 1944. The nearer one, which is the same piece shown in the preceding photograph, has just fired a round. This action occurred nine days after the beginning of the US invasion of Leyte.

Taken at the same firing position and time as in the preceding photo, this image shows an artilleryman holding the right side of a loading tray, carrying a projectile up to the 155 mm gun during a firing mission near Dulang, Leyte. Depending on the type of projectile, the weight the two men had to carry on a loading tray to the breech of the Long Tom was between 95 and 100 pounds.

Each member of a 155 mm gun crew had a carefully orchestrated role in the operation of the gun. As seen in another photo of 155 mm artillerymen in action near Dulag, Leyte, the no. 4 and no. 6 crewmen are carrying a loading tray with a 155 mm projectile on it, while the man standing on the right trail, either no. 2 or no. 3, is checking the gunner's quadrant, a portable instrument for measuring the elevation or depression of the gun and checking the adjustment of elevation-sighting devices. To the left is the gunner, operating the traversing handwheel.

A row of six 155 mm Long Toms are in a firing position in a clearing in a palm grove near Ormac, Luzon, Philippines, in November 1944. The guns were serving with Battery B, 983rd Field Artillery. At the time the photo was taken, the guns were firing at a concentration of Japanese troops 10 miles away; they were reinforcements who had been landed on a beach. Smoke is issuing from the muzzles of several of the Long Toms toward the far end of the line.

A 155 mm gun is blasting at Japanese troops on the Carigara front on Luzon in the Philippines on November 4, 1944. The gun was assigned to Battery B, 983rd Field Artillery. A large stack of 155 mm projectiles are to the rear of the gun.

A lone 155 mm Long Tom outside Hébronval, Belgium, fires a shell at a German position on January 14, 1945. The gun, assigned to Battery C, 981st Field Artillery, has white cloth wrapped around the barrel and parts of the carriage for camouflage in the snow.

In the Gabbiano area of Italy on January 13, 1945, members of a South African heavy artillery unit attached to the 5th Army are shelling German forces. These artillerists had to contend with freezing temperatures and deep snow in the pursuit of their mission.

A 155 mm gun from Battery B, 985th Field Artillery Battalion, is poised to fire with direction from a forward observer in an RAF Spitfire near Loiano, Italy, on January 22, 1945. The gun has a thoroughly applied coat of white paint, for winter camouflage.

While being towed to a new firing position during a blizzard near Loiano in the northern Apennines in Italy on January 9, 1945, this 155 mm Long Tom of the 985th Field Artillery Battalion went out of control, crashing into the Mack NO truck in the background.

On January 17, 1945, two whitewash-camouflaged 155 mm Long Toms (the barrel of one of them is faintly visible beyond the lone soldier toward the right) are supporting an attack by the 35th Infantry Division east of Bastogne, Belgium.

A Mack NO prime mover is hauling a 155 mm gun from the 561st Field Artillery Battalion to a firing position near Beiler, Luxembourg, on January 29, 1945. The gun and the truck have well-worn coats of water-soluble whitewash camouflage.

This is the first of a series of three photos documenting a contact-repair team from the 16th Ordnance Medium Maintenance Company replacing a damaged right equilibrator on a 155 mm gun in the 9th US Army area in Germany on January 27, 1945.

The contact-repair team has removed the damaged right equilibrator from the 155 mm gun and is carrying the replacement equilibrator to the gun. The man leaning against the tire is straddling a nitrogen bottle, to be used in replenishing the nitrogen in the equilibrator.

Ordnancemen are hauling on a rope during the replacement of the right equilibrator. The damaged equilibrator they removed from the gun carriage is in the foreground. Because of the dangers of the nitrogen content of equilibrators, repairs were restricted to experts.

The crew of a 155 mm Long Tom prepares it for firing on New Caledonia on January 31, 1945. The gunner is adjusting his sight; two men are lifting the right front spade from its holder on the side of the trail. The man behind the breech is handling the barrel-retraction cable.

Crewmen from the 981st Field Artillery Battalion are loading a 155 mm gun during a shelling of retreating German troops at Heppenbach, Belgium, on February 3, 1945. The gun had a mix of whitewash and white cloth wrapped around the tube for camouflage.

White cloth tape has been wound around the tube of this 155 mm Long Tom with the 981st Field Artillery Battalion at Heppenbach, Belgium, on February 3, 1945. The crewman below the muzzle has dumped a bucket of cleaning solution into the tube.

This 155 mm gun from the 559th Field Artillery Battalion, 90th Division, rolled over near Steffeshausen, Belgium, on February 1, 1945, when its prime mover missed a curve in the road, killing four members of the crew. The Mack NO prime mover is a twisted wreck.

A thoroughly whitewashed 155 mm Long Tom from the 731st Field Artillery Battalion, III Corps, is in a sandbagged emplacement in a field north of Wiltz, Luxembourg, on February 2, 1945. The crew's tent is erected in the background, near the gun.

Two artillerymen on New Caledonia in March 1945 are holding a clamping bracket, used to hitch the trails of a 155 mm gun to the Mack NO prime mover. This bracket had been modified by adding two grab handles, to prevent injuries to crewmen's hands.

Five members of a crew from Battery A, 264th Field Artillery Battalion, are cleaning the bore of an 8-inch howitzer M1 after a fire mission against German troops across the Rhine River near Bad Godesberg, Germany, on March 2, 1944.

Crewmen of a 155 mm Long Tom from the 244th Field Artillery Battalion, 26th "Yankee" Division, 3rd US Army, prepare to put their piece into action outside Gelnhausen, Germany, on March 30, 1945. Behind the gun is an M4 high-speed tractor.

On March 31, 1945, an M4 high-speed tractor is towing a 155 mm Long Tom off a landing craft at Keise Shima, off the coast of Okinawa. Written in script on the front of the M4 are "Rosie Lee," "Lucky," and "Tigers." To the rear is an ammo trailer, hitched to the gun.

A crew from the 420th Field Artillery Group is emplacing a 155 mm gun in a sandy firing pit on Keise Shima on March 31, 1945. An ace-of-diamonds card is painted on the tube. From Keise Shima, 155 mm guns could shell Japanese positions on southern Okinawa.

A 155 mm gun crew from the 420th Field Artillery Group contends with thick coral sand while emplacing the piece on March 31, 1945. The 155 mm guns landed on Keise Shima on March 31 and would bombard enemy positions on Okinawa on D-day, the following day.

Crews of three 155 mm Long Toms in prepared firing pits on Keise Shima on March 31, 1945, are loading their pieces. The closest gun has "Extra Duty" inscribed on the tube. In a draw in the center distance is an M4 high-speed tractor. Projectiles are piled in the foreground.

This photo is the first of two documenting a 155 mm Long Tom whose tube exploded during a fire mission on April 19, 1945, killing two and wounding four of the crew. The photos were taken in the vicinity of Lauf, Germany, the day after the accident.

A GI looks over the wreckage of the 155 mm gun. This piece was serial number 863. When it exploded, it was firing a supercharge with a high-explosive projectile. The gun already had fired over 3,000 rounds since being put into service. The suspected cause of the accident was thought to have been a faulty M1-type breech ring, because other 155 mm guns with that type of breech ring had suffered similar explosions. The gun was photographed where it had been in action at the time of the explosion, with camouflage netting still rigged around it.

A 155 mm Long Tom of the 530th Field Artillery is in a sandbagged emplacement during a pause in fighting in a mountainous locale in the II Corps area of Italy on April 6, 1945. Another Long Tom is in a similarly sandbagged emplacement in the background.

The same 155 mm gun and gun emplacement seen in the foreground in the preceding photograph are viewed from a nearer perspective on April 6, 1945, as a crewman inserts a propellant charge into the breech. The loader is wearing heavy-duty gloves.

On Okinawa on April 9, 1945, a member of an 8-inch howitzer M1 crew is preparing to dump a bucket of water into the bore, for cleaning purposes. Other members of the crew, visible under the camouflage net, are ready to swab the barrel with a bore-cleaning brush.

Battery B, 749th Field Artillery Battalion, was the first unit to operate the 8-inch howitzers M1 in the Pacific, and one of that unit's 8-inch pieces is seen here deployed in a firing position a half mile northeast of Futenma, Okinawa, on April 20, 1945.

The MI firing platform gave the 155 mm gun all-around fire on a level, stable plane. The bottom carriage pivoted on a bolster at the center of the platform, and the trails moved on the round. This example on Angaur was manned by the 45th Coast Artillery Battalion.

On Angaur in the Palau Islands on April 29, 1945, at the same site shown in the preceding photo, members of Battery A, 45th Coast Artillery Battalion, assemble an M1 firing platform in the foreground, while a 155 mm gun occupies a platform in the background.

Members of Battery A, 45th Coast Artillery Battalion, are assembling the track of an M1 firing platform on Angaur on April 29, 1945. Correctly emplacing the platform entailed much digging, leveling of ground, emplacing support planks, and backfilling.

A Long Tom crew from Battery A, 465th Field Artillery Battalion, pose for a photo while shelling Japanese positions on a ridge 500 yards away, near Ballete Pass, Luzon, on May 25, 1945. All members of the crew hailed from Boston, Massachusetts.

The 155 mm Long Toms and the 8-inch howitzer M1s saw action again during the Korean War. Here, a line of four 8-inch howitzers M1 from the 1st Cavalry Division are emplaced and ready for action near Taegu, Republic of Korea, on September 15, 1950.

The following sequence of photos seems to be at the same location as in the preceding photo, but original labels identify the place as near Waegwan, which is close to Taegu. Here, a mixed crew of Americans and Koreans clean an 8-inch howitzer bore.

American and South Korean crewmen load a projectile into an 8-inch howitzer near Waegwan, Republic of Korea. The South Korean crewmen seem to have been the ones in these photographs who have white Xs marked on the sides of their M1 helmets.

In a final photo from Waegwan, dated September 17, 1950, members of the 17th Field Artillery Battalion have just fired an 8-inch howitzer M1 at Communist forces. The piece is in full recoil, and some crewmen shout or cover their ears to minimize the blast effect.

During the Korean War, training of heavy artillery crews continued at Fort Sill, Oklahoma. This crew from Battery A, 780th Field Artillery Battalion, is firing an 8-inch howitzer M1 at that facility on November 24, 1950. The projectile is visible in flight.

The no. 2 8-inch howitzer of Battery B, 780th Field Artillery Battalion, US 8th Army, is firing on Communist troops on Hill 940, also called "Bloody Ridge," in support of an attack by the 9th Infantry, 2nd Infantry Division, in Korea on September 2, 1951.

At the same firing position as seen in the preceding photo, the no. 4 8-inch howitzer M1 of Battery B, 780th Field Artillery, fires a shell toward enemy forces on Bloody Ridge, September 2, 1951. A large embankment had been bulldozed to the front of the emplacement.

Members of Battery C, 17th Field Artillery Battalion, US 8th Army, fire an 8-inch howitzer against Communist forces on Hill 355 near the Imjin River in Korea on October 31, 1951. A red band with the field artillery's crossed-cannons insignia is on the barrel.

A 155 mm Long Tom of the 469th Field Artillery is being prepared for firing on Aggressor forces in support of XV Corps during Exercise Long Horn at Fort Hood, Texas, on March 28, 1952. The gun enjoys camouflage protection from the surrounding trees.

An 8-inch howitzer M1 nicknamed "PERSUADERS," assigned to Battery A, 17th Field Artillery Battalion, fires on Communist forces near Mount Baldy, outside Chorwon, Republic of Korea, on August 23, 1952. Propellant packing tubes are in the foreground.

410724

The same 8-inch howitzer M1 shown in the preceding photo is viewed from a closer perspective while firing at enemy troops on the other side of Mount Baldy on August 23, 1952. The fire mission was in support of an attack by the 2nd US Infantry Division.

Crewmen from Battery B, 145th Field Artillery Battalion, are preparing to fire a 155 mm Long Tom in Korea in August 1952. The loader is inserting a supercharge—an augmented propellant charge—for purposes of calibrating the muzzle velocity.

Col. Ray O. Welch, commander of the Pueblo Ordnance Depot in Colorado, stands below the breech ring of a 155 mm Long Tom at the depot on March 17, 1954. The big gun was being prepared for outdoor storage at the facility. The gun and carriage have been freshly painted: red-lead primer and enamel buckets are on the ground. The telescoping joints on the equilibrators have been taped over.

Members of the crew of a 155 mm gun apply evergreen branches to the piece for camouflage during Exercise Flashburn, training maneuvers at Fort Bragg, North Carolina, on March 24, 1954. The camouflage has rendered only part of the barrel and a tire visible from this perspective. These artillerists and the gun were part of Battery B, 540th Field Artillery.

This photo is the first of a series of four images documenting the test firing of an 8-inch howitzer at the Yuma Test Station, Yuma, Arizona, on November 22, 1954. The premise of the test was to evaluate the performance of temperature-controlled ammunition.

Civilian employees of the Yuma Test Station are loading an 8-inch projectile into the breech during test firing of a howitzer at the Arms and Ammunition Range. Out of the photo to the left, a man stands ready to push the projectile home with a rammer staff.

A technician sights though the bore of an 8-inch howitzer at the Yuma Test Station, checking the alignment of the howitzer's tube with velocity coils on the towers in the background, which will measure the velocity of the projectile as it passes through them.

The 8-inch howitzer is loaded and ready for firing at the velocity coils in the background, at the Yuma Test Center on November 22, 1954. In the right foreground are numerous 8-inch projectiles, which will be fired in the ensuing tests.

A crewman standing on a heavy limber M5 is pulling the cover off the muzzle of a 155 mm gun M59 with "BLOOD" and "US ARMY" stenciled on the tube. The two men on the sides of the bogie wheels are using wrenches to lower the carriage to firing position.

A Mack M125 10-ton truck (G-792), registration number 5B1587, is towing an 8-inch howitzer M115 (formerly M1) during a training exercise in West Germany in 1963. On the front of the truck and on the side of the cargo body are signs in English and German warning that explosives are aboard. The unit markings on the bumper of the truck refer to the twenty-third vehicle in the line of march of Battery B, 1st Battalion, 83rd Field Artillery, 7th Army.